# The Teleportation Glitch

Story by Sarah Fallon

Illustrations by Mario Gushiken

**The Teleportation Glitch**

Text: Sarah Fallon
Publishers: Tania Mazzeo and Eliza Webb
Series consultant: Amanda Sutera
  Hands on Heads Consulting
Editor: Kirsty Hine
Project editor: Annabel Smith
Designer: Jess Kelly
Project designer: Danielle Maccarone
Illustrations: Mario Gushiken
Production controller: Renee Tome

**Acknowledgements**
From the author Sarah Fallon:
For my parents. They told me I could be
anything I wanted to be and gave me the
tools to try.

NovaStar

**Cengage Learning Australia**
Level 5, 80 Dorcas Street
Southbank VIC 3006 Australia
Phone: 1300 790 853
Email: aust.nelsonprimary@cengage.com

For learning solutions, visit **cengage.com.au**

Printed in China by 1010 Printing International Ltd
1 2 3 4 5 6 7 28 27 26 25 24

*Nelson acknowledges the Traditional Owners and Custodians
of the lands of all First Nations Peoples. We pay respect
to Elders past and present, and extend that respect to
all First Nations Peoples today.*

# Contents

## Chapter 1

# Far, Far Away

I was hanging out on the oval with my best friend, Tegan, during lunch. She was showing me how the teleportation app on her new smartwatch worked.

"You just put your destination in here. Tap here and away you go," she said.

"That is so awesome!" I said. "I really hope Mum and Dad have got me one."

Today was my birthday, and that night Tegan was coming over for a special birthday dinner.

More than anything, I wanted the latest smartwatch. Then I could teleport to anywhere in the blink of an eye. Just like all my friends. No more running late for school because I'd slept in. No more missing out on beach trips because Mum and Dad were too busy to drive me.

I'd been pleading with my parents for the new smartwatch for months, but it wasn't looking likely. Every time I brought it up, they said no. They thought the teleportation technology was too new and untested. They didn't trust it, and they thought my old smartwatch still worked just fine. My watch was so ancient, it was embarrassing.

To be honest, I didn't really understand how the teleportation technology worked. Our teacher, Ms West, had explained that there are satellites on a space station that communicate with the smartwatches. Together, they turn people into tiny bits of information. Then, they move that information to another location and put it back into human form! Or something like that. (I'm more into art than science.)

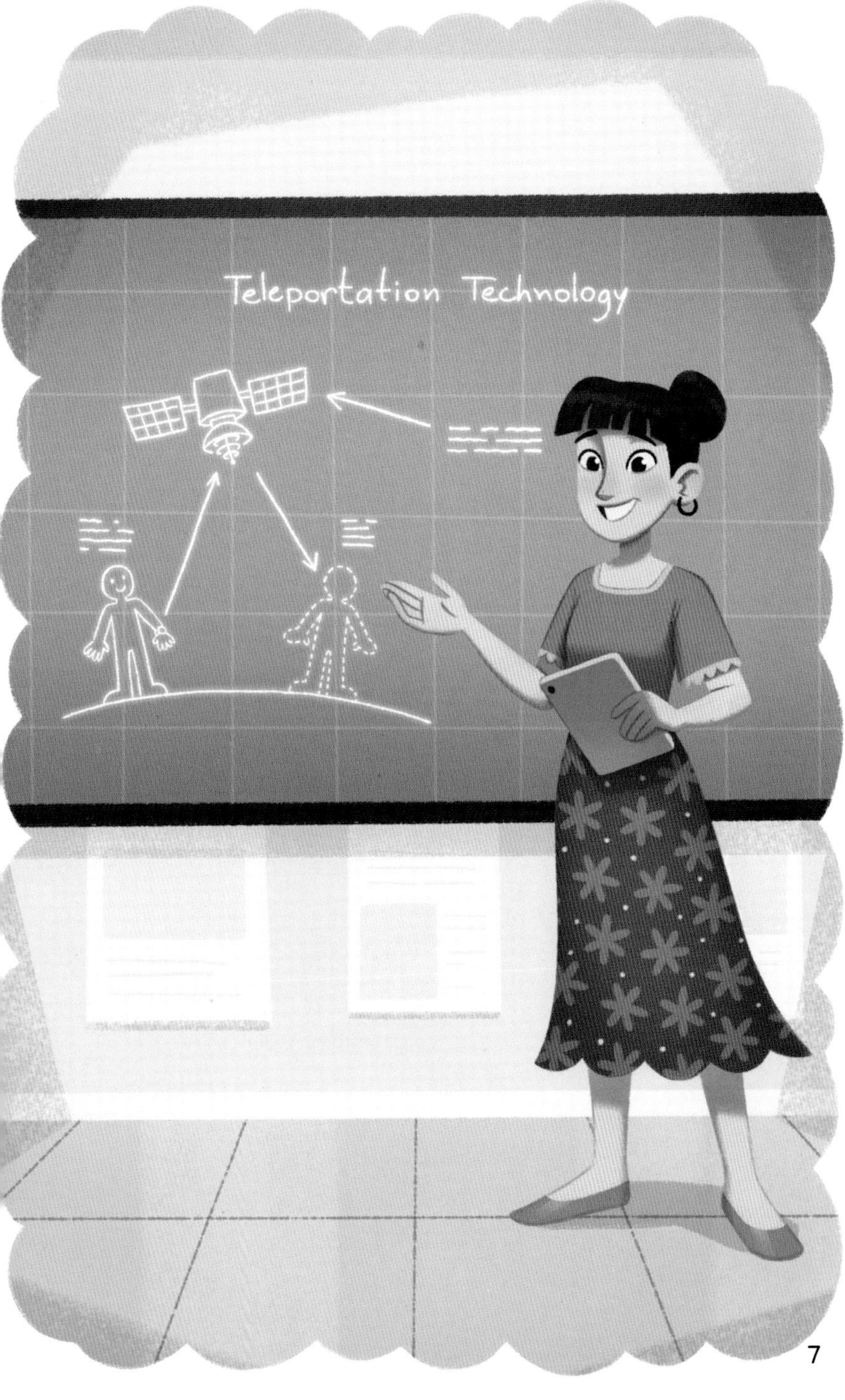
Teleportation Technology

"Do you think ..." I began, eyeing Tegan's watch. "Do you think I could have a go?" Borrowing Tegan's smartwatch was probably the closest I'd ever get to teleporting.

Tegan frowned. "Um, I guess so. Just don't go too far."

I squealed with excitement. "Thank you! I'll just teleport to the other side of the school and back."

"Okay," said Tegan. "Give me your watch, then you can send me a pic when you get there."

"Awesome," I said, as we exchanged watches. I put in my destination, just like Tegan had shown me.

I grinned at Tegan.

She smiled back. "Have fun, Maeve."

Then I tapped the teleport button on the bottom of the screen.

My body hummed. It felt like pins and needles from head to toe. Tegan and the oval faded into a jumble of pixels.

Then the pixels cleared, and I was standing in a corridor with curved walls and no windows. This wasn't any part of the school I'd ever seen.

I took a step forward. My legs felt like jelly and my head swam. I leant against the wall. Was this a normal part of teleportation? None of my friends had ever mentioned feeling dizzy or sick before. Moving slowly, with one hand against the wall, I turned a corner. It was a dead end, but there was a big round window from floor to ceiling.

My stomach dropped. Through the window, I could see Earth.

It was a blue ball in the distance surrounded by millions of stars.

I definitely wasn't at school any more. I was in space!

# Chapter 2

# Out of Battery

My heart was racing. How would I get home? I started tapping frantically on the watch face. I selected "Return journey" in the teleportation app, and just as I was about to hit "Teleport", the screen went black.

"Argh!" I groaned. Tegan never fully charged her things. I sank to the floor and leaned my head against my knees. Accidentally teleporting to space was just about the worst thing that could have happened to me. My parents would never get me a new smartwatch now. That's if I even made it home for dinner ... or at all.

I breathed in and out slowly. I kept taking deep breaths until the tightness in my chest eased, then I raised my head to look around. Focusing on details always helped me calm down.

There weren't many details in the corridor, except out the window, and I certainly didn't want to look out there again. Other than that, there were some panels and switches, and on the opposite wall was a map.

Teleportation Hub Space Station 01275

CONTROL FACILITY

YOU ARE HERE

I stood up and went to look at the map more closely. It was labelled "Teleportation Hub: Space Station 01275" and there was a big green dot on one side of it that read: "You are here". So that explained where I was – I was at the space station that communicated with the smartwatches.

That also explained why everything felt weird and wobbly. There must be artificial gravity here that was keeping me from floating around. Ms West had tried explaining that to us as well. Astronauts spent ages preparing for this environment, and I got dizzy just riding a merry-go-round.

I went to take a photo of the map with Tegan's watch, then remembered the watch was out of battery. I would never be able to keep track of which way to go now.

I wondered what people used to do before there were such things as smart phones and smartwatches. Then I remembered!

I stuffed my hands in my pockets and pulled out a pencil and a scrap of paper I'd been doodling on at lunch. I copied the map, complete with a dotted line from the "You are here" dot to the room labelled "Control Facility". That seemed like the most likely place to find someone in charge.

My legs were still shaky, but I followed my dotted line as best I could. The space station was made up of circular rooms connected by long, narrow corridors. I had to pass by each room as I followed the corridor. Thankfully, they were all unlocked and labelled above the wheel-like door handle, so I knew I was going in the right direction.

I came to a door labelled "Recreation Module". Checking my map, I saw the dotted line I had drawn ran straight through it. I spun the handle and the door flew open. On the other side was a bookshelf full of novels and board games, a ping pong table and a boy sitting on a couch.

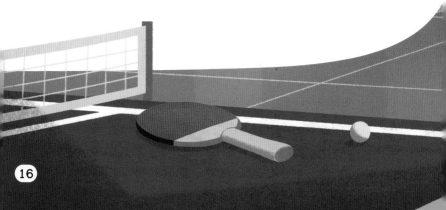

# Chapter 3

# Someone to Help

The boy jumped when he saw me.
His eyes were bulging out of his head.
"Who are you? How did you get here?"

"My name's Maeve," I said. "I teleported here from Earth."

"What? That's not possible."

"It was an accident and now I can't get home. My watch, I mean my friend's watch, ran out of battery." It felt good to have someone to tell; someone who might be able to help.

"Did you say your friend's watch?" He raised an eyebrow.

"Yeah, she let me borrow it, so I could try teleporting."

"Seriously? The latest smartwatch is synced to your own body. You can't just use someone else's watch. What do they teach you at school?"

"Aren't you in school too?" I said, annoyed.

"Well, yeah, but I'm homeschooled. Or space-station schooled. My parents work here for six months of the year. When I was little, I would stay with my grandparents on Earth, but for the last few years they've brought me along. It means I know a lot about teleportation. Name's Harjan." He held out his hand.

I shook it. "Must be cool living in space."

"Most people think so, but you can't do anything or go anywhere. I just want to ride my BMX and go hiking again."

"Why don't you just teleport?" I asked.

"I can't," replied Harjan. "Teleportation has only been created for use on Earth. Or it's supposed to be. My parents, and the rest of the team, have been running experiments all day today, though. They've been opening teleportation communication lines between Earth and the space station every half hour."

Harjan frowned and then continued, "They must have done it just when you tried to teleport. That, and the watch not being synced to your body, must be what caused this weird teleportation glitch."

Harjan explained things just like a teacher.

"Right. I just need to get back to school before lunch finishes. I don't want to get in trouble on my birthday," I said.

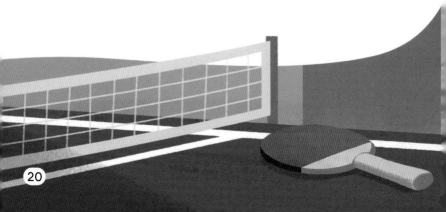

"Oh," he said. "Happy birthday."

"Thanks. So ... can someone here help me?" I asked.

"All the scientists are locked up in the Experiment Module," Harjan said.

Great, I thought. How long would I have to wait? I was going to get in trouble for sure.

Then Harjan smiled. "I can help."

# Chapter 4

# A Way Home

Harjan looked at his smartwatch. "My parents are planning on opening the communication line one more time today, in about ten minutes. We've got to get to the Control Facility, charge your friend's watch and reset it to sync with your body before then. They only open the line for thirty seconds, so we have to be set to go as soon as they do. Are you ready?"

"I can't move very fast," I said, starting to feel panicky again.

"Oh right, the artificial gravity here would be weird if you haven't been trained for it. We can walk. I'm sure we'll still make it." He held my hand, and I took a few deep breaths.

"Ready?"

"Yes."

Harjan led the way out of the Recreation Module and down another corridor. I wanted to run. Every bit of my body wanted to get there as fast as possible, but as soon as I increased my pace, I felt dizzy and had to slow down. Finally, we reached a door labelled "Control Facility".

Harjan checked the time. "The shutdown will start soon," he said. He spun the wheel and the door swung open.

As soon as I stepped into the room, Tegan's watch dinged to life.

"This whole room is a wireless charger," Harjan explained.

"That's handy. What do we do now?" I asked.

"Hold out the watch. I'll sync it with your body. Don't forget to re-sync it when you give it back to your friend."

I nodded, holding out my wrist. Harjan talked me through each step as he tapped on the face of Tegan's smartwatch. I watched and listened closely, so I could recreate the steps for Tegan when I got home.

"Okay, they're about to open the line," said Harjan. "Hopefully the watch has enough battery to handle the teleportation."

"What if it doesn't?" I asked.

"Best not to think about it." Harjan laughed nervously, and my stomach tied in knots. "Let's do this." He opened the teleportation app on Tegan's smartwatch.

"Thank you," I said, suddenly.

"Of course," Harjan grinned. "This is the most exciting thing that's happened in the whole six months I've been here."

"When do you come back to Earth?" I asked.

"Next week," he said.

"Come and visit me," I said, hoping he would. "I'll take you hiking."

Harjan grinned again. "I'd like that." He punched the destination into the app. "I know where you'll be." Then he tapped the teleportation button and everything around me faded into pixels.

## Chapter 5

# Birthday Dinner

I was standing on the oval in front of a very angry Tegan. "Where have you been?" she shrieked. "I was just about to tell a teacher! You didn't even send me a pic."

I shook my head, hoping to clear the dizziness. "It's not my fault your watch ran out of battery!"

"Oh." Tegan's hands dropped from her hips. "Whoops. How did you get back?"

I was about to start telling her the whole story when the bell rang for the end of lunch. "Quick," I said, "I'll tell you on the way."

I finished the story as we filed into class.

"That Harjan guy sounds cool. Do you really think he'll visit?" Tegan asked.

"I hope so. He was nice, but he could live on the other side of the world for all I know. When he's not living on a space station, that is."

"He can always just teleport. Or you can, if your parents get you the watch," Tegan said.

"To be honest, the whole experience has put me off teleporting a bit. Maybe a bike would be a better present. A BMX even," I said, as we took our seats.

Ms West gave us a warning look and we fell silent. We could talk more at home tonight.

My parents picked Tegan and me up after school. My birthday dinner was just what I needed after the wild adventure at lunch. Dad had made my favourite meal and mum had bought a delicious lemon tart from the bakery down the road.

After we finished eating and Tegan and I were rolling around on the couch with full bellies, Mum appeared in the lounge room with a present. It was a small box wrapped in blue and green paper with a yellow bow.

"Are you ready for your surprise?" Dad asked, as Mum handed me the present.

I held my breath as I unwrapped the box.
It was exactly what I'd hoped for.
The new smartwatch.

"Dad and I had a talk, and we changed
our minds about getting you a smartwatch,"
said Mum.

"Oh, thank you," I said, still a little unsure
I wanted it any more.

My parents seemed disappointed by my reaction, so I jumped off the couch and gave them a big hug. If I just followed the rules Harjan had told me, there shouldn't be any more glitches anyway.

"Just don't teleport anywhere silly," Mum and Dad said together.

"Trust me, I won't if I can help it," I said.

A new smartwatch, a new friend and a trip to space. I couldn't have asked for a better birthday.